AMERICA THE
Beautiful

Katharine Lee Bates ★ Illustrated by Chris Gall

L B

LITTLE, BROWN AND COMPANY

New York   Boston

For my grandmother,

Elizabeth Keith Olmstead

Illustrations copyright © 2004 by Chris Gall

Little, Brown and Company

Hachette Book Group
237 Park Avenue, New York, NY 10017
Visit our website at www.lb-kids.com

Little, Brown and Company is a division of Hachette Book Group, Inc.
The Little, Brown name and logo are trademarks of Hachette Book Group, Inc.

First Paperback Edition: June 2010
Originally published in hardcover in April 2004 by Little, Brown and Company

ISBN 978-0-316-08338-6

10 9 8 7 6 5 4 3 2 1

SC

Printed in China

The illustrations for this book were done by hand engraving clay-coated board,
then digitizing with Adobe Illustrator for adjustments and color.
The text was set in Deepdene Italic and Deepdene.

America the Beautiful

Katharine Lee Bates

Samuel A. Ward

O beau - ti - ful for spa - cious skies, For am - ber waves of grain, For

pur - ple moun - tain maj - es - ties A - bove the fruit - ed plain! A -

mer - i - ca! A - mer - i - ca! God shed His grace on thee And

crown thy good with broth - er - hood, From sea to shin - ing sea!

O beautiful for spacious skies,
For amber waves of grain,

For purple mountain majesties
Above the fruited plain!

America! America!
God shed His grace on thee

And crown thy good with brotherhood
From sea to shining sea!

O beautiful for pilgrim feet,
Whose stern, impassioned stress

A thoroughfare for freedom beat
Across the wilderness!

America! America!
God mend thine every flaw,
Confirm thy soul in self-control,
Thy liberty in law!

O beautiful for heroes proved
In liberating strife,

Who more than self their country loved
And mercy more than life!

America! America!
May God thy gold refine
Till all success be nobleness
And every gain divine!

O beautiful for patriot dream
That sees beyond the years

Thine alabaster cities gleam
Undimmed by human tears!

America! America!
God shed His grace on thee

And crown thy good with brotherhood

From sea to shining sea!

About the Artwork

Lighthouses have always served as beacons of security, guiding wayward travelers to safety. West Quoddy Head Light in Maine sits on the easternmost piece of American soil.

Appreciation of the natural wonders of the land, great or small, begins during childhood.

In 1930, the nation was fed by more than six million small farms nationwide. Today, family farms have dwindled in number, but the legacy of America's agricultural heritage remains.

The view of Pike's Peak from the Garden of the Gods, Colorado Springs, Colorado. From the summit in 1893, Katharine Lee Bates was inspired to write "America the Beautiful."

For many, the change of seasons in a small town embodies the romance of American rural life.

Around 1805, the Shoshone Indian named Sacagawea—along with her son, affectionately referred to as "Pompy"—began to help explorers Lewis and Clark navigate the Missouri River and find passage to the Pacific Ocean.

Millions of immigrants from all over the world have contributed to the rich tapestry of American culture. During the country's densest period of immigration, from 1892 to 1924, most made the long journey aboard ships.

The travel trailer has given many families the opportunity to see our country's great natural wonders. Exciting stories about the pioneer Daniel Boone's adventures led to the popularity of the coonskin cap.

The statue of Lady Justice dates back to antiquity and has long been used to symbolize our courts. The blindfold stands for impartiality, the scales for fairness, and the sword for enforcement.

During World War Two, the men known as the Tuskegee Airmen were the first African-American flying unit in the U.S. military. They destroyed more than 260 enemy aircraft and won more than 850 medals.

The heroes of September 11, 2001. On that tragic day, more than 400 firemen, policemen, and rescue workers gave their lives in the service of their fellow citizens. New York firefighters pulled a battered American flag from the rubble and hoisted it high.

The Statue of Liberty stands more than 300 feet above ground and is perhaps our most recognizable symbol of freedom and liberty. Her torch is coated with 24-karat gold leaf.

The Saturn V rocket booster lifts *Apollo 11* to the moon. On July 20, 1969, Neil Armstrong and Edwin "Buzz" Aldrin became the first humans to walk on the moon.

A window washer takes a break on a hot summer day. Finished in 1930, the Chrysler Building in New York City has 77 stories and a variety of stainless-steel ornaments derived from the design of automobiles of the time.

Family time and leisure time are some of the great gifts that many Americans treasure.

On May 10, 1869, the East and West Coasts were finally connected by railway at Promontory Summit, Utah. The ceremony included the locomotives "Jupiter," representing the Central Pacific Railroad, and the "119," representing the Union Pacific Railroad.